Cricket

by Vaishali Batra

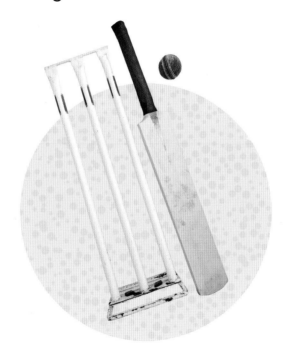

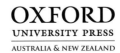

OXFORD
UNIVERSITY PRESS
AUSTRALIA & NEW ZEALAND

I get a sun hat.

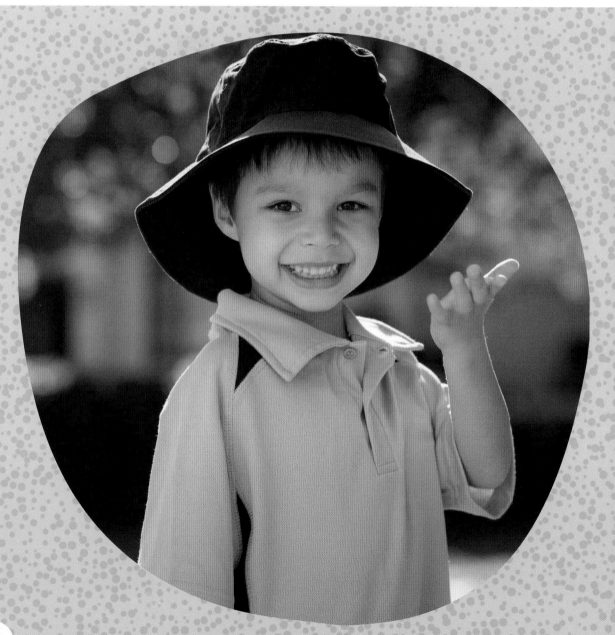

I pick up a big bat.

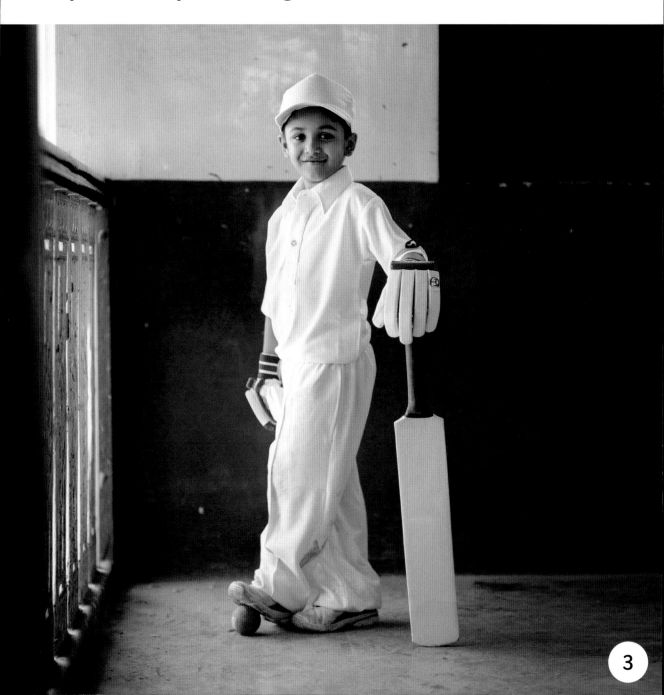

I toss it.

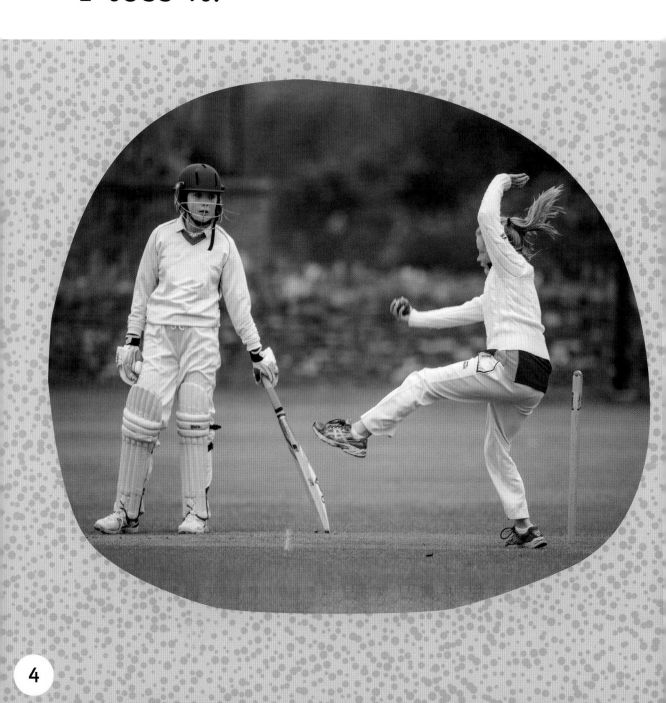

I hit it back.

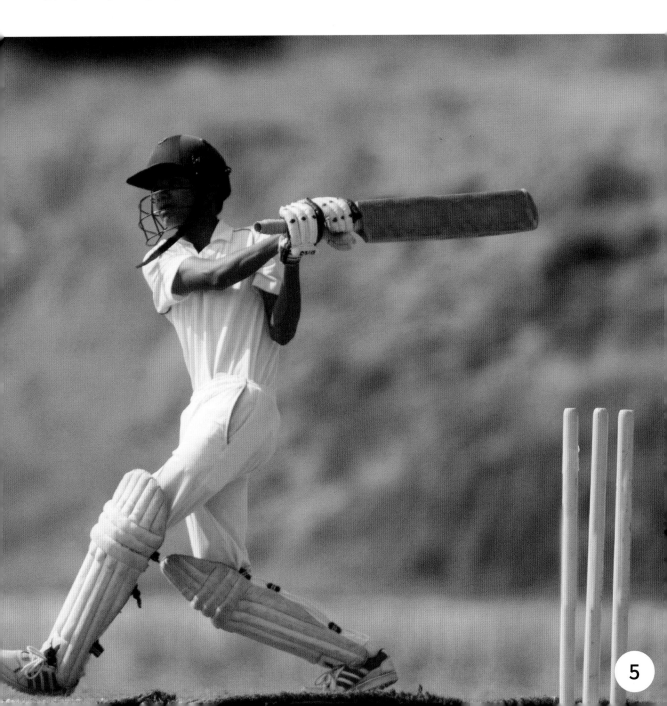

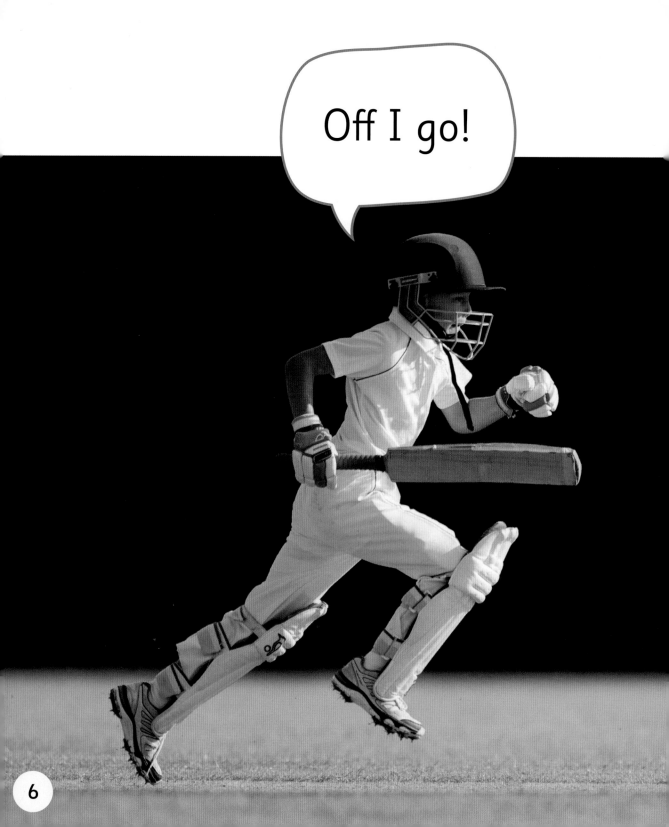

I get a run.

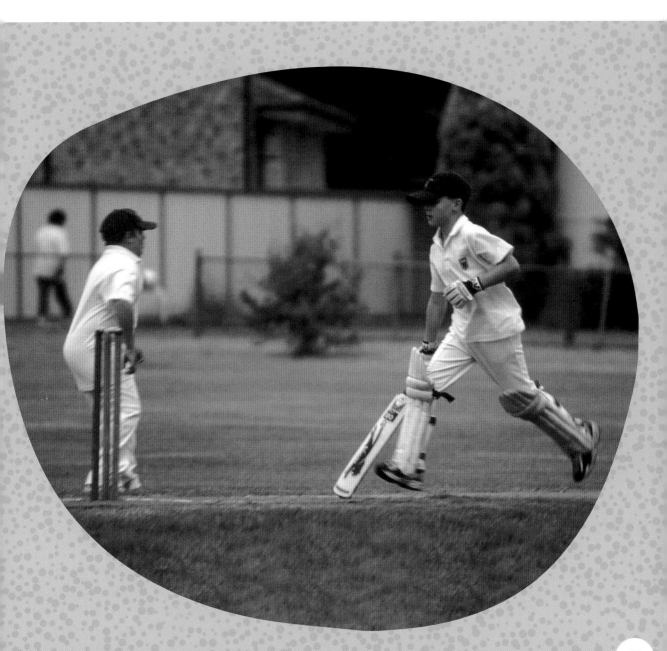

I miss it.

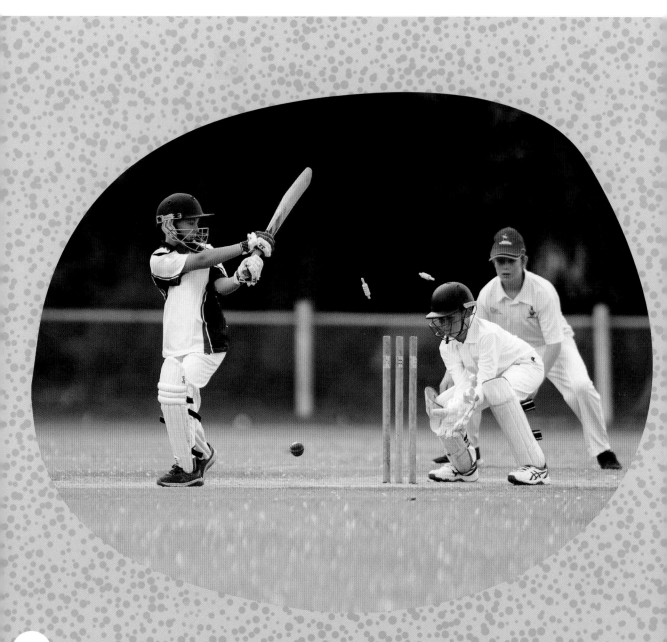

I run and pick it up.

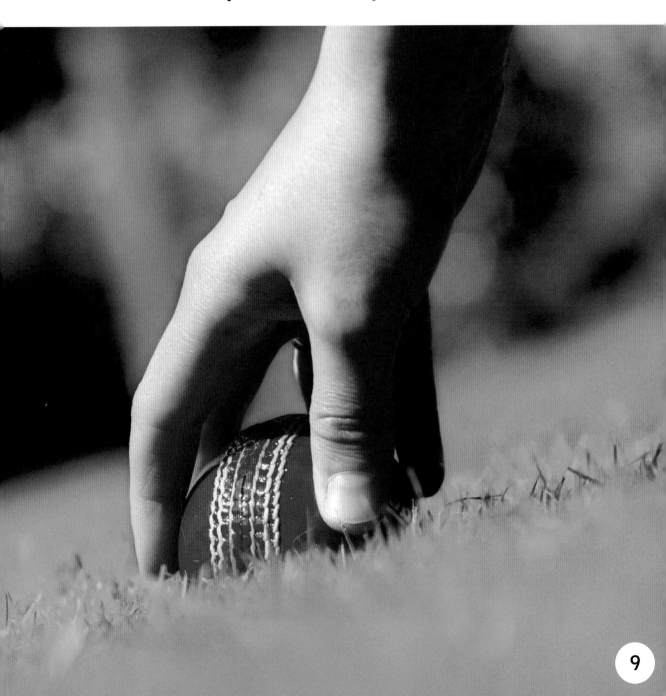

I hit it up.

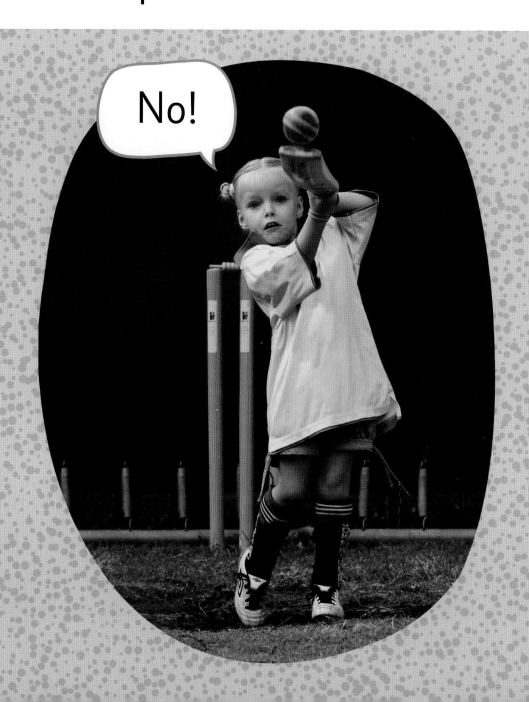

I fell.

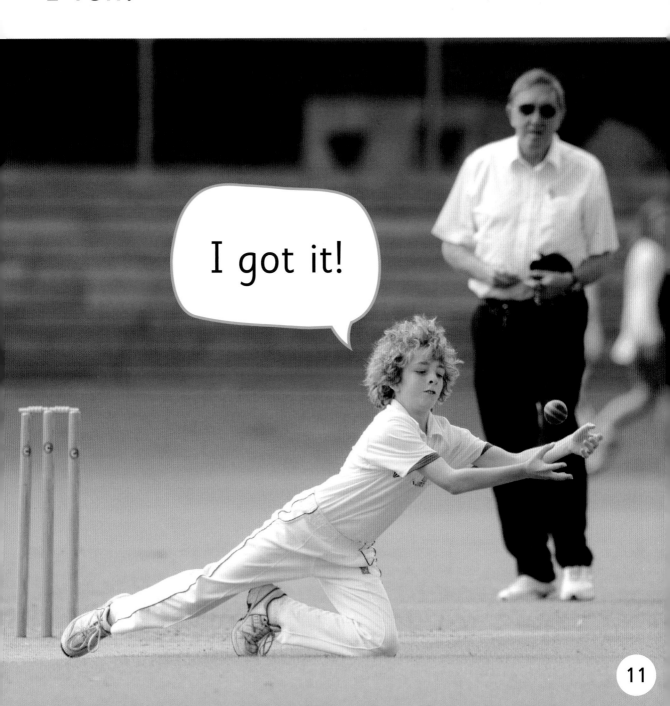

I got it!

It is lots of fun.

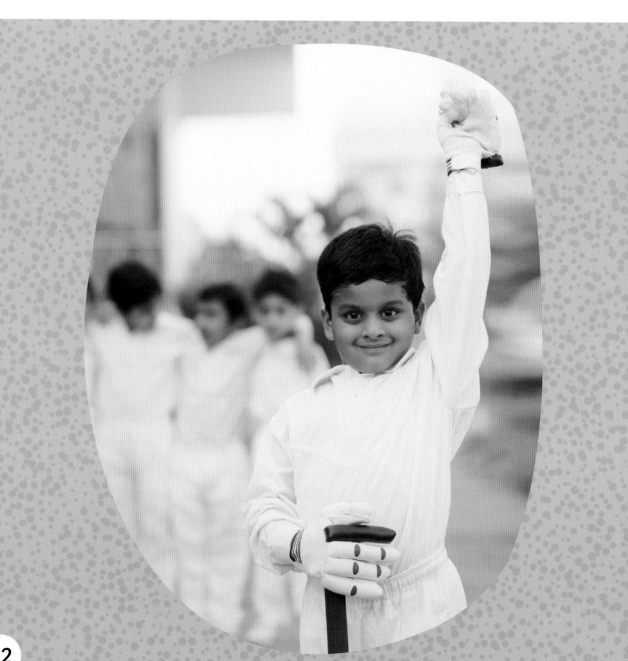